THE UNCOMMON MINISTER

Steps To
Achieving
Your Goals In
Your Ministry

VOLUME 7

MIKE MURDOCK

TABLE OF CONTENTS

The Uncommon Minister, Volume 7
Copyright © 1999 by Mike Murdock
ISBN 1-56394-106-6

Published by The Wisdom Center
P. O. Box 99 • Denton, Texas 76202

≈ 1 ≈

BECOME A WORSHIPPER.

Praise creates internal enthusiasm.

It is 8:35 a.m. this Thursday morning. Went to bed about 3:00 a.m. this morning. Was awakened about twenty minutes ago to a pounding in my spirit of the song, "I will bless the Lord at all times...His praise shall continually be in my mouth."

This is one of the secrets of the ministry.

You must learn about thankfulness.

The evil forces, the demonic spirits, have one desire. Satan wants to rob God of *any moment of pleasure.* Every moment that praise does not exude and flow from your mouth, it is a theft, robbing God of what is rightfully His.

1. *You* Must Personally Bless The Lord. Nobody else can do it for you. You must praise Him. Your *people* cannot do it for you.

2. You *Must* Bless The Lord. You must purpose in your heart. Make a decision. *Determine* to do it. Become tenacious and persistent about it. Set your mind in agreement with it.

3. You Must *Bless* The Lord. He's blessed you! Everything around you shows blessing. His health and healing flows through your being. Your mind throbs with motivation. Your heart is full of dreams and goals. He is worthy of your blessing Him... honoring Him...bringing Him glory.

4. You Must Bless *The Lord.* Many request

attention. Others pull at your strength, your attention, your life, your time, and your energy.

Letters are pushed in my father's face..."Make sure Dr. Murdock gets this personally." Telephone calls come to my friend in the middle of the night. "Tell Dr. Mike this for me."

But, I refuse to permit anybody around me *to become the priority focus of my life*. I was created for Him...*for Him*. When He dominates my life, *only then* do I have something worthwhile to give to others, minister to them and feed them. If I permit others to become mere parasites in my life, they will not be sustained. *Both* of us will be destroyed.

If God is my focus, everything else I do *will multiply and prosper*. Others will increase *because of it*.

You must bless *the Lord*. He is the precious Holy Spirit Who walks besides you. Your Advisor and Counselor. Your Best Friend. The One Who knows all things. He *remembers* every word that Jesus spoke, and He reminds you so that you can "enter into the life of Christ."

Spirit focus will not always be easy. Others may *always attempt* to be the focus. They need attention. They require fueling and energy from you.

They interpret withdrawal as rejection. Yet, you must become so conscious that if God is not your focus, your mind *loses* its peace. Your heart *loses* its joy. Your life *loses* precision and sense of purpose.

5.   You Must Bless The Lord *At All Times*. How nice it would be if you could simply "segment a part of the day" and give Him total focus, and then move on with your tasks. But there is something about the currents of this life. *The whirlpool of busyness*.

Satan won't let you have a special time to "get alone with God" without a fight.

Nobody else around you will permit it either.

The very ways of this world keep you sucked in, emptied out, and with no time to just focus on Him and His presence.

Here's your solution. *Bless the Lord at all times. Every moment.* Each hour. Every day. Make the precious Holy Spirit your total focus and obsession. Others will simply get the *overflow* of His flowing in your life.

At all times. When you are looking at contracts to sign from a realtor, whisper His name. Say quietly, "I love You, precious Holy Spirit." Pray in tongues over and over continuously. "But ye beloved, building up yourselves praying in the Holy Ghost" (Jude 20).

At all times. When I am shaving and trying to get things together in the morning to head to the office, I do not wait until I get into my private place of prayer. Bless Him *at all times.*

You see, when your own dreams and goals become your focus, agitation will erupt. When you are thwarted, someone slows you down or does not follow an instruction, you may become disoriented.

When *others* become your focus, you may become sickened inside when their words wound you. Their countenance may show disdain and contempt for you. Your own family may appear to have been "disappointed in you" because you failed to fulfill their unspoken expectations of you.

The precious Holy Spirit must become your total focus.

My Minister Friend, you cannot "leave" the

road and head down a winding path to accommodate every emotional scar and emptiness of your people.

You must *stay with God.*

When you stay with God, *The Hungry for God will find you also.*

When you stay with God, *The Thirsty will observe you and fellowship will begin.*

Bless the Lord at all times.

Become A Worshipper.

It is One of the Secrets of The Uncommon Minister.

⟅ 2 ⟆

BE WILLING TO PREACH TRUTHS THAT MAY ANGER OTHERS.

Truth always infuriates somebody.

The preaching of Jeremiah angered people. "Now Pashur the son of Immer the priest, who was also chief governor in the house of the Lord, heard that Jeremiah prophesied these things. Then Pashur smote Jeremiah the prophet, and put him in the stocks that were in the high gate of Benjamin, which was by the house of the Lord" (Jeremiah 20:1,2).

Here is a remarkable photograph of a preacher's son hating the words of a man of God. His own father was a priest, but he despised the gospel he heard from *another* minister.

Men of God obey God. Whatever the cost.

The messenger does not always carry encouraging news. Many years ago, a preacher declared, "If a man is a true prophet of God, it will be good news and edifying to you."

Wrong.

True prophets often carry tragic news. Jeremiah is an example. "And thou, Pashur, and all that dwell in thine house shall go into captivity: and thou shalt come to Babylon, and there thou shalt die, and shalt be buried there, thou, and all thy friends, to whom thou hast prophesied lies" (Jeremiah 20:6).

6 Facts Every Minister Should Remember About Preaching

1. *Preaching Often Intimidates Those With Wrong Motives.* Be willing to do as Jesus did: expose the hypocrisy of Pharisees around you.

2. *Preach The Return Of Jesus.* Do it even when millions say that He has delayed His coming. "And saying, Where is the promise of His coming? for since the fathers fell asleep, all things continue as they were from the beginning of the creation" (2 Peter 3:4).

3. *Preach The Healing Power Of Jesus.* Do it even when some teach erroneously that God is using sickness and disease to correct you. "But He was wounded for our transgressions, He was bruised for our iniquities: the chastisement of our peace was upon Him; and with His stripes we are healed" (Isaiah 53:5).

4. *Preach The Miracle Power Of God.* Do it even when others say that was for the early disciples only. "The Lord is not slack concerning His promise, as some men count slackness; but is longsuffering to us-ward, not willing that any should perish, but that all should come to repentance" (2 Peter 3:9).

5. *Preach The Word.* Do it even when others seem to have more fascinating experiences and testimonies. "The prophet that hath a dream, let him tell a dream; and he that hath My Word, let him speak My Word faithfully. What is the chaff to the wheat? saith the Lord. Is not My Word like as a fire? saith the Lord; and like a hammer that

breaketh the rock in pieces?" (Jeremiah 23:28,29).

6. *Preach To Expose False Prophets.* Do it regardless of how clever, cunning and intellectual they appear to be. Jeremiah did. "I have not sent these prophets, yet they ran: I have not spoken to them, yet they prophesied. But if they had stood in My counsel, and had caused My people to hear My words, then they should have turned them from their evil way, and from the evil of their doings" (Jeremiah 23:21,22).

Be Willing To Preach Truths That May Anger Others.

It is One of the Secrets of The Uncommon Minister.

⇒ 3 ⇐

KNOW YOUR MATE.

------⇒●⇐------

Your mate is affecting you.
Your mate is affecting your ministry.
Your mate is affecting your people.
Your mate grows your weakness or your strength.
Your mate multiplies your agitation or your peace.
Your mate is helping create the climate of torture or triumph at your house. "Two are better than one; because they have a good reward for their labour" (Ecclesiastes 4:9).
You must invest the time to understand and know your mate if you want to maximize your life and ministry.

5 Facts Ministers Should Know About Their Mates

1. *Know The Wounds Of Your Mate.* A pastor sat in my home weeping. "My wife has not touched me in six months," he wept. "Mike, I can't take it much longer. I want to be held, touched and loved."
A childhood experience of molestation is a powerful influence that often goes undetected while destroying many marriages.
2. *Know The Fears Of Your Mate.* A young wife tearfully admitted that her father's infidelity and

unfaithfulness to her mother had left her embittered. She falsely accused her husband when any behavior reminded her of her father.

3. *Know The Closest Friends Of Your Mate.* Your children are always affected by their friendships at school. They react differently to you after they have been with their friends. Your mate will, also.

"I wouldn't put up with that from my husband," a friend told a pastor's wife. She returned home with volcanic anger. Her friend had only heard one side of the argument. Yet, she embraced the counsel of that uninformed friend.

4. *Know Those Who Counsel Your Mate.* Never, never, never again will I permit someone I love to receive counsel without me being present. I was shocked and horrified to hear the counsel received by someone I loved several years ago. *Don't send your mate or children to a counselor you do not know well.* In fact, I would urge you to sit in on every counseling session to protect those you love from unwise and distorted counsel.

5. *Know The Weaknesses Of Your Mate.* Lust? Lying? Imagination? Jealousy? Inferiority? Prevention is often possible when you understand the flaws and weaknesses of your mate. You can protect and build a wall around them.

Know Your Mate.

It is One of the Secrets of the Uncommon Minister.

∞ 4 ∞

ALWAYS EXIT RELATIONSHIPS GRACIOUSLY.

Few relationships last forever.

But, it is important to exit every Door of Friendship properly. You cannot enter the next season of your life with joy unless you exit your present season *correctly.*

Recognize when a relationship is ending. Permit it to close with grace and dignity.

Jesus finished His work on earth. He cried out from the cross, "It is finished!" Salvation was complete. Redemption had taken place. He had paid the price for the sins of man. Three days later, the resurrection would occur. He would return to the Father where He would make intercession for you and me. He finished *properly*—with the approval of the Father.

Solomon finished the Temple. It was an incredible feat. Some have valued the temple today at over 500 billion dollars. Solomon was respected, pursued and celebrated. He *completed* what he started.

Paul finished his race. He declared that he had fought a good fight, kept his course and finished the race. He was a success in the eyes of God. He made his exit from earthly ministry with grace, dignity and passion. Your ministry will be a collection of *Beginnings.* Your ministry will also be a collection of *Exits.* You may not stay in your present church or position forever. You will likely leave your present position. George Barna says the average tenure for a pastor today is 21 months.

Close every Door gently. Do not slam Doors. Do not kick Doors. Do not yell at Doors. They are Doors *through which you may want to return again* in the future days of your ministry. Your attitude during *your exit* often determines whether you will ever walk back through the Door again.

Close every Door with forgiveness. Unforgiveness is poisonous. It is the cancer that will destroy you from within. Release others to God. Permit Him to do the penalizing or correcting. Like Joseph, recognize that the ultimate plan of God will bring your promotion. "And we know that all things work together for good to them that love God, to them who are the called according to His purpose" (Romans 8:28).

Close every Door with kindness. If a church member leaves with cutting and bitter words, refuse to become bitter. "Let all bitterness, and wrath, and anger, and clamour, and evil speaking, be put away from you, with all malice: And be ye kind one to another, tenderhearted, forgiving one another, even as God for Christ's sake hath forgiven you" (Ephesians 4:31-32).

Close every Door with your promises fulfilled. Finish *what you promise.* Complete your vows.

Whatever the cost. I test the integrity of others by simply asking myself, "Did he do what he said he would do?" "When thou vowest a vow unto God, defer not to pay it; for He hath no pleasure in fools: pay that which thou hast vowed. Better is it that thou shouldest not vow, than that thou shouldest vow and not pay" (Ecclesiastes. 5:4,5).

The Law of Completed Vows can bring you much peace. Sometimes, people can lose you in the Forest of Words. When they have left, questions can leave you baffled, confused and puzzled. Yet, it is simple. Apply the Law of Completed Vows. Forget the blaming, complaining and accusations. This Law reveals everything you need to know about another person.

Close every Door with integrity. Few will do it. People are rarely angry for the reason they tell you. Employees rarely leave for the reason they explain. Much is never discussed. Deception is deadly. It begins when you deceive *yourself.* Then, those around you. Always be honest to others about *the reason* for the Doors closing. It is unnecessary to provide *every* detail. But, it is important that the details you offer are *truthful*.

Close every Door with courage. It is not always easy to close a Door. Sometimes, when you have been involved in a special friendship, it has brought comfort. It has stopped loneliness. It has relieved the burden of emptiness. So, closing a Door requires courage to face the future without that person. Remember who your true Source is for every gift you need. It is not another person. It is the Holy Spirit, the gift of the Father to you.

He *opens* Doors.
He *closes* Doors.

*Close every Door with expectation of
supernatural promotion.* The Law of Increase
indicates tomorrow is a promotion. God uses the
opposite principle of satan. The kingdom of hell
operates on the Law of the Sweet and Bitter. Satan
offers you the sweet to seduce you. Then, the
bitterness destroys. Delilah offered the fragrance of
seduction, leaving Samson as the blinded, laughing
stock of the Philistines.

God operates the Law of the Bitter-Sweet. God
offers you the bitter first. Then, rewards you with
the sweet. Jesus invited us to "take up your cross
and follow Me." Then, the promise was quite clear:
if you suffer with Him, you will reign with Him.

Job experienced the Law of the Bitter-Sweet.
He went through the bitter season but came out with
double blessings. "And the Lord turned the captivity
of Job, when he prayed for his friends: and also the
Lord gave Job twice as much as he had before" (Job
42:10).

When you close Doors gently, you can *expect
favor to flow again.* It happened to Job. "Then came
there unto him all his brethren, and all his sisters,
and all they that had been of his acquaintance before,
and did eat bread with him in his house: and they
bemoaned him, and comforted him over all the evil
that the Lord had brought upon him: every man
also gave him a piece of money, and every one an
earring of gold" (Job 42:11).

When you close Doors gently, *expect financial
multiplication.* It happened to Job. "So the Lord
blessed the latter end of Job more than his beginning:
for he had fourteen thousand sheep, and six thousand
camels, and a thousand yoke of oxen, and a thousand
she asses" (Job 42:12).

Close every Door at the proper time. Do not close it in a fit of anger. Do not close the Door because of a misunderstanding that erupts. Do not close it because someone *recommends* that you exit. Close the Door in the *Timing of the Holy Spirit.* "To everything there is a season, and a time to every purpose under the heaven...a time to get, and a time to lose; a time to keep, and a time to cast away:.. a time to keep silence and a time to speak" (Ecclesiastes 3:1-8).

God always brings you out of a place to bring you into another place. A young man sat in my kitchen a few weeks ago. I was quite concerned. He wanted a position in my ministry. I asked him about his relationship with his previous boss, my pastor friend. He avoided the issue continuously. In fact, I had to ask him the question four or five times before I got a partial answer. At the end of the conversation, he explained his financial dilemma. He had left a job before ever securing another one. I explained to him how foolish this was. If God was moving him, He would tell him the place where he was to go.

When God told Elijah to leave the brook, Zarephath was scheduled. (Read 1 Kings 17.)

When the Israelites left Egypt, Canaan was the determined destination. (See Exodus 13.)

So, close every Door with God's timing. When you close Doors gently, news will travel. Good news.

Always Exit Relationships Graciously.

It is One of the Secrets of The Uncommon Minister.

≈ 5 ≈

DEVELOP THE DAILY
HABIT OF ORDER.

Order is the accurate arrangement of things.

Order is placing an item where it belongs. Order is keeping your shirts, ties and shoes in the appropriate place in your closet.

Each small act of your life increases order or disorder around you.

The purpose of order is to increase *productivity* and create *comfort.* When you walk into a room of order, you want to *stay.* Things are "right." You feel clean, energized and happy. When you walk into a room of clutter and disorder, an unexplainable agitation begins. Sometimes, you are unable to even name it or understand it. But, *you were created for order*, and anything that slows you down emotionally or mentally will become a distraction.

When you increase order in your ministry, you will increase your productivity. Filing cabinets, trays on the desk, and special places for folders make it easier to get your tasks done *on time.* Have you ever shuffled paper after paper in search of a bill? Of course! When you finally located the bill, you were agitated and angry. It affected your entire day. *Disorder influences your attitude* more than you could ever imagine.

Everything you are doing is affecting order in

your life. Think for a moment. You get up from your breakfast table. Either you will leave your plate on the table, or you will take it to the sink. The decision you make will either increase the order or disorder around you. (Leaving it on the table increases your work load and creates disorder. Taking it to the sink *immediately* brings *order.*)

It happened last night for me. I took off my suit coat and laid it over the chair. I didn't really feel like taking it over to the closet and hanging it up. But, realizing that I was going to hang it up sooner or later, I walked over to the closet and hung up my coat. I immediately increased order around me.

Every moment you are increasing order or creating disorder around your ministry. Small, tiny actions can eventually produce chaotic situations.

Every person around you is increasing order or disorder. Some people have an *attitude* of disorder. They are unhappy unless everything is in disarray and cluttered. Others refuse to work in such an environment. Their productivity requires organization.

Somebody has said that the arrangement of things in your garage reveals much about your mind. Somebody asked me once, "Does this mean if I do not have a garage, that I really do not have a mind either?" (Smile!) I certainly hope that is not the case, but I am certain psychologists have come to some pretty accurate conclusions.

Why do we permit disorder?

Many of us were raised with those who are disorganized. Large families, busy lifestyles, or small cramped apartments can contribute to your attitude.

Some have unusual creativity and simply are uninterested in keeping order around them. Busyness, moving from place to place, keeps you disorganized. Your mind is on where you are *going* rather than where you *are*.

6 Helpful Hints On Order

1. *Recognize The Long-Term Chaos And Losses That Disorder Will Create.* If this continues, your momentum will eventually destroy you and your productivity. Successes will become fewer.

2. *Take A Long Hard And Serious Look At Your Personality.* What can you do to take steps toward change?

3. *Ask Others Who Are Gifted In Organization To Assist You And Keep You On Course.* I read where Donald Trump said a few days ago that he hired one woman whose entire job is to keep things in order around him.

4. *Don't Berate Yourself And Become Overly Critical Because Of Your Lack Of Knowledge, Giftings Or Ability To Keep Things In Order.*

5. *Recognize Those Who God Puts Close To You Who Can Correct Things Around You And Keep Things In Order.*

6. *Don't Try To Justify Disorder Around You.* Relax, and take a small step today toward order.

It is commendable that you are planning to take an entire week of your vacation to put everything in order in your house next summer. However, I suggest you begin *this very moment* taking some steps to put things in place here in the room.

Twenty minutes can make a major difference. Little hinges swing big doors. You can get anywhere you want to go if you are willing to take enough small steps.

Develop The Daily Habit Of Order.

It is One of the Secrets of The Uncommon Minister.

∾ 6 ∾

ALWAYS KEEP A SMALL TAPE RECORDER IN YOUR HAND.

Talking is faster than writing.
Someone has said that you can talk six times faster than you write. I *always* keep note paper and pen handy. *Always.* But, it is far easier and more productive to dictate in a small microcassette than it is to write longhand on my legal pad. Admittedly, some of my notes excite me more when I can see them written large in my own handwriting while using a black Sharpie pen. But, when there is a flood of ideas and thoughts pouring through me, I consider the small tape recorder to be a gift from God for every achiever.

I have only known two friends in my entire life who keep a microcassette recorder with them at all times. Others claim to have them "somewhere in my office." Or somewhere "down here in my briefcase." But, they are not accustomed to using a recorder on a daily basis.

Recording frees your mind from the stress of memory. When you want to remember something, you will often find yourself continuously playing it over and over in your mind...hoping you will not forget it. Consequently, your mind cannot be free for great *ideas*, a season of unusual creativity, or be used in immediate conversations with total focus. Why? Subconsciously, you are trying to *remember* something, to do it later or tell someone about it. People try to remember everything. We keep lists, tie strings around our fingers, or picture something we want to remember.

But, I began to produce ten times more with my life when I created the *habit* of keeping a microcasstte recorder with me...*every moment* of my life.

Develop the habit of keeping it conveniently close. At first, it may be uncomfortable. When I started keeping my microcassette recorder in my pocket, it seemed a little odd, awkward and even cumbersome. After I saw the many pages of material that I produced because of it, it became a joy. It was a constant reminder that great thoughts and ideas flowed through me.

Don't feel obligated to constantly record. I've had my microcassette with me for two days and never used it once. Activity around me was so hectic and my schedule so full, everything else required too much from me. But, it was accessible. Handy. Convenient. If I did require it, it was there. Anyhow, I was forming the *habit* of dictating.

Making each moment produce is one of the greatest secrets of an uncommon ministry. Thousands keep waiting for that "perfect time" that they are going to take off a few days or weeks to produce a book, plan a project or design their house.

A decade can pass without any of it occurring, unless you understand how to *turn each moment into a miracle.*

Use your recorder constantly.

Always Keep A Small Tape Recorder In Your Hand.

It is One of the productivity Secrets of The Uncommon Minister.

≈ 7 ≈

NEVER REBEL AGAINST A FINANCIAL DELIVERER GOD SENDS TO YOU AND YOUR PEOPLE.

———⟫●⟪———

Your ministry has not been forgotten by God.
Nobody loves you more than the Person who created you. Your fears are known by Him. Your tears matter to Him.

12 Facts You Should Remember About Financial Deliverers

1. *When Your Ministry Is Hurting Financially, God Will Bring A Financial Deliverer Toward You.* Every moment of your life God is scheduling miracles. Like currents of blessing, they flow into your life and through your ministry.

Your prison will have a door.

Your river will have a bridge.

Your mountain will have a tunnel.

But, you must find it. Look for it. Listen for it. Search for it. Believe that it exists. "There hath no temptation taken you but such as is common to man: but God is faithful, who will not suffer you to be tempted above that ye are able; but will with the temptation also make a way to escape, that ye may be able to bear it" (1 Corinthians 10:13).

2. *You Must Pursue Those God Is Using To Fuel Your Financial Faith.* There are wonderful men and women of God who carry *financial* anointings. They can unlock your faith. It may involve a four-hour drive to their crusade. *It is important that you honor, treasure and pursue that Mantle.* Listen to their tapes. Read their books. Listen to their heart.

They have tasted failure.

They know how to get out of trouble.

They know what sleepless nights are like.

They have defeated the demons of fear.

That is why they are qualified to mentor you and your people.

Some ministers will never taste their financial harvest because they are sitting under leaders who fuel their doubts and unbelief. They listen to *church members* who continuously discuss the economic problems on the earth, hard times and how difficult life is.

▶ *The Voice You Keep Hearing Is The Voice You Will Believe.*

▶ *The Voice Your People Keep Hearing Is The Voice They Will Believe.*

Ten spies infected millions of Israelites with their unbelief and doubt. When they talked about the giants, the people forgot about the Grapes of Blessing.

What you *talk* about increases.

What you *think* about becomes larger.

Your *mind* and your *mouth* are *magnifiers* of anything you want to grow.

Two spies came back from Canaan with faith,

victory, and the ability to overcome giants. Their names were Joshua and Caleb. They had been with God. They had seen the giants, but were not afraid. They had seen the grapes and decided to become champions. They had experienced too many days in the wilderness to be satisfied with failure. They became Champions of Faith. Joshua became the leader of Israel after the death of Moses. Caleb became known for "taking his mountain." Oh, the rewards of faith are so sweet! The taste of victory stays in your mouth so long!

You must discern the Joshuas and Calebs around you. Find faith food. Listen for faith talk. Sit under it. Listen and absorb. Something within you will grow. Something within your people will grow.

I receive much inspiration from the story of Elijah and the widow in I Kings 17. I never tire of this incredible Well of Wisdom.

She was hurting. Devastated. Starving. She was one meal from death.

That's when a Financial Deliverer was sent into her life.

He did not criticize her.

He did not coddle her.

He did not sympathize with her.

He knew *how* to get her *out of trouble.*

She had to *listen* to him.

She had to *discern* that he was a man of God.

She had to be *willing* to follow his instructions, regardless of how ridiculous and illogical they seemed to her natural mind.

3. *Another Man Of God Often Holds The*

Golden Key To Your Financial Deliverance. Can you discern him? If you respect his anointing, chains will fall off. Blindness will disappear. Your eyes will behold the Golden Path to blessing.

If you become critical, resentful, and rebellious, you will abort the most remarkable Season of Miracles God has ever scheduled into your life. *Nobody else can discern this man of God for you.* You must do it yourself. *Nobody else can force you to obey this man of God.* Your heart must be soft and broken enough to follow God.

4. *You May Receive Only One Opportunity To Obey The Instruction Of A Financial Deliverer That Brings Your Breakthrough.* Remember Nabal only received one opportunity to feed and bless the army of David.

5. *You Must Recognize Greatness When You Are In The Presence Of It.* It will not always demand attention. Jesus was many places where He was undiscerned, undetected and unrecognized. His own family did not perceive His mantle or His assignment.

6. *You May Have To Seek Out The Man Of God Before He Pursues You.* You see, he is not really needing you. You need him.

Read the incredible story of Saul and his servant, who had lost their donkeys. They were so disturbed *until the servant remembered that a man of God lived in the area.* The servant knew the power of giving an offering. They made the decision to find the Prophet Samuel. The rest of the story is absolutely remarkable. When they came into the presence of Samuel, the anointing of the prophet began to flow toward Saul.

They *sowed* an offering.

They *believed* a man of God.

That encounter with Samuel catapulted Saul into the kingship of Israel.

7. *Somewhere, There Is A Man Of God With The Golden Key To Your Door Of Blessing.* Your responsibility is to *find* him, *discern* him and *obey* his instructions.

Several years ago, my assistant listened to me share the miracle of the "Covenant of Blessing," the sowing of the $58 Seed.

My first encounter was in Washington, DC, when the Holy Spirit instructed me to plant a Seed of $58 to represent the 58 kinds of blessings I had found in Scripture. My obedience launched an incredible parade of miracles into my personal life and ministry. I have told about this everywhere.

My assistant was a fine young man who loved God. Faith came alive as he listened to me tell my experience. I instructed him and others present in that service to give their Seed "an Assignment."

"Write on your check where you need the harvest in your own life," I instructed.

He planted his Seed of $58, and wrote "better family relations" on his check. Seven amazing miracles happened following his Seed of Obedience.

▶ His mother accepted Christ within 14 days.

▶ His two sisters accepted Christ within 14 days.

▶ His daughter accepted Christ within 14 days.

▶ He was able to spend a week with two of his daughters he had not seen in five years.

► He was able to have a meal with his entire family, which had not happened in 15 years.

► His 86 year old father accepted Christ within 90 days.

► His oldest sister, who had run away from home 48 years earlier, was found! She came back home for a family reunion. Nobody had seen or heard from her for those 48 long years. She had been thought to be dead.

Everyone of these miracles happened within 90 days of his sowing his Seed of $58.

He had simply followed the instruction of a man of God.

Almost everywhere I go, I ask those who need miracles to plant a Seed. A specific Seed. Often, I invite believers to plant a Seed of $58. Sometimes, it is more, depending on the leading of God in the services. The miracles are incredible. I get letters from everywhere relating the supernatural intervention of God *following their acts of obedience.*

A woman in Knoxville, Tennessee, approached me with a tall husband by her side. "Remember that Seed of $58?" she asked.

"Yes."

"This is him!" He had been away from Christ. Within a few days after her Seed, he came to church with her and gave his heart to God!

8. *The Financial Deliverer God Sends To You May Not Be Packaged As You Desire.* John the Baptist had an appearance many could not tolerate. But, God was with him. *God's greatest gifts do not always arrive in silk.* He often uses burlap bags to package His best prizes. "The Lord seeth not as man seeth; for man looketh on the outward appearance, but the

Lord looketh on the heart" (1 Samuel 16:7).

9. *The Financial Deliverer God Sends Into Your Church May Have An Abrasive Or Uncomfortable Personality.* If you could have heard Isaiah or Ezekiel, you might be shocked at some of the strong language that poured from their lips.

10. *The Financial Deliverer God Sends With A Special Challenge To Your Church May Even Be A Social Misfit.* God often uses foolish things to confound the wise. You will not discern them through the hearing of the ear nor the seeing of the eye. "But God hath chosen the foolish things of the world to confound the wise; and God hath chosen the weak things of the world to confound the things which are mighty" (1 Corinthians 1:27).

11. *You Will Only Discern Your Financial Deliverer By The Spirit Of God Within You.* "Believe in the Lord your God, so shall ye be established; believe His prophets, so shall ye prosper" (2 Chronicles 20:20).

12. *When You Begin To Acknowledge The Word Of The Lord Coming From Proven And Established Servants Of God, The Flow Of Miracles Will Multiply And Increase Toward You And Your People.*

Never Rebel Against A Financial Deliverer God Sends To You And Your People.

It is One of the Secrets of The Uncommon Minister.

WISDOM KEYS FOR AN UNCOMMON MINISTRY.

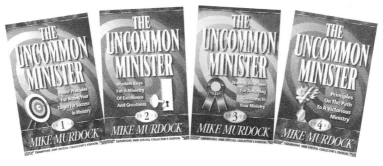

Complete your personal library of
"The Uncommon Minister" Series. These first seven
volumes are a must for your ministry reading.
Practical and powerful, these Wisdom Keys will
enhance your ministry expression for years to come.

ITEM	TITLE	QTY	PRICE	TOTAL
B107	The Uncommon Minister, Volume 1		$5.00	$
B108	The Uncommon Minister, Volume 2		$5.00	$
B109	The Uncommon Minister, Volume 3		$5.00	$
B110	The Uncommon Minister, Volume 4		$5.00	$
B111	The Uncommon Minister, Volume 5		$5.00	$
B112	The Uncommon Minister, Volume 6		$5.00	$
B113	The Uncommon Minister, Volume 7		$5.00	$
All 7 Volumes of The Uncommon Minister			$35.00	$

Mail To: **The Wisdom Center** P.O. Box 99 Denton, TX 76202 940-891-1400	Add 10% For Shipping	$
	(Canada add 20% to retail cost and 20% shipping)	$
	Enclosed Is My Seed-Faith Gift For Your Ministry	$
	Total Amount Enclosed	$

SORRY NO C.O.D.'S

Name _____
Address _____
City _____
State _____
Zip _____ Telephone _____

❏ Check ❏ Money Order
❏ Visa ❏ Master Card ❏ Amex
Signature _____
Exp. Date _____
Card No. _____

THE
WISDOM
CENTER

———— **Quantity Prices for** ————
"The Uncommon Minister" Series

1-9	=	$5.00 each
10-99	=	$4.00 each (20% discount)
100-499	=	$3.50 each (30% discount)
500-999	=	$3.00 each (40% discount)
1,000-up	=	$2.50 each (50% discount)
5,000-up	=	$2.00 each (60% discount)

WISDOM 12 PAK

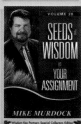

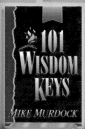

THE MASTER SECRET OF LIFE IS WISDOM
Ignorance Is The Only True Enemy Capable Of Destroying You (Hosea 4:6, Proverbs 11:14)

▸	1.	MY PERSONAL DREAM BOOK	B143	$5.00
▸	2.	THE COVENANT OF FIFTY EIGHT BLESSINGS	B47	$8.00
▸	3.	WISDOM, GOD'S GOLDEN KEY TO SUCCESS	B71	$7.00
▸	4.	SEEDS OF WISDOM ON THE HOLY SPIRIT	B116	$5.00
▸	5.	SEEDS OF WISDOM ON THE SECRET PLACE	B115	$5.00
▸	6.	SEEDS OF WISDOM ON THE WORD OF GOD	B117	$5.00
▸	7.	SEEDS OF WISDOM ON THE ASSIGNMENT	B122	$5.00
▸	8.	SEEDS OF WISDOM ON PROBLEM SOLVING	B118	$5.00
▸	9.	101 WISDOM KEYS	B45	$7.00
▸	10.	31 KEYS TO A NEW BEGINNING	B48	$7.00
▸	11.	THE PROVERBS 31 WOMAN	B49	$7.00
▸	12.	31 FACTS ABOUT WISDOM	B46	$7.00

Wisdom Is The Principal Thing

Book Pak
WBL-12 / **$30**
(A $73 Value!)

The Wisdom Center

ORDER TODAY!
www.thewisdomcenter.cc

1-888-WISDOM-1
(1-888-947-3661)

THE WISDOM CENTER • P.O. Box 99 • Denton, Texas 76202

Somebody's Future
Will Not Begin Until You Enter.

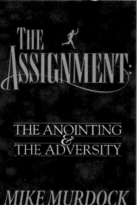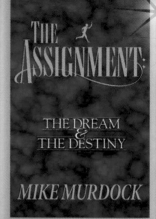
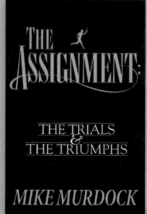

**THIS COLLECTION INCLUDES 4 DIFFERENT BOOKS CONTAINING
UNCOMMON WISDOM FOR DISCOVERING YOUR LIFE ASSIGNMENT**

▶ **How To Achieve A God-Given Dream And Goal**

▶ **How To Know Who Is Assigned To You**

▶ **The Purpose And Rewards Of An Enemy**

Wisdom Is The Principal Thing
Book Pak
WBL-14 /$30
Buy 3-Get 1 Free
($10 Each/$40 Value!)
The Wisdom Center

The Secret Place

Library Pak

Songs from the Secret Place

Over 40 Great Songs On 6 Music Tapes
Including "I'm In Love" / Love Songs From The Holy Spirit
Birthed In The Secret Place / Side A Is Dr. Mike Murdock
Singing / Side B Is Music Only For Your Personal Prayer Time

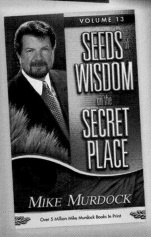

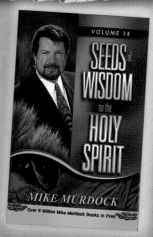

Seeds of Wisdom on the Secret Place

4 Secrets The Holy Spirit Reveals In The Secret Place / The Necessary
Ingredients In Creating Your Secret Place / 10 Miracles That Will
Happen In The Secret Place

Seeds of Wisdom on the Holy Spirit

The Protocol For Entering The Presence Of
The Holy Spirit / the greatest day of my life and
What Made It So / Power Keys For Developing Your
Personal Relationship With The Holy Spirit

Wisdom Is The Principal Thing
Book/Tape Pak
SP PAK-001 /$30
Six Audio Tapes & Two Books
(A $40 Value!)
The Wisdom Center

Getting Past The Pain.

Wisdom For Crisis Times

Master Keys For Success In Times of Change

Mike Murdock

- ▶ 6 Essential Facts That Must Be Faced When Recovering From Divorce
- ▶ 4 Forces That Guarantee Career Success
- ▶ 3 Ways Crisis Can Help You
- ▶ 4 Reasons You Are Experiencing Opposition To Your Assignment
- ▶ How To Predict The 6 Seasons Of Attack On Your Life
- ▶ 4 Keys That Can Shorten Your Present Season Of Struggle
- ▶ 2 Important Facts You Must Know About Battle & Warfare
- ▶ 6 Weapons Satan Uses To Attack Marriages

Wisdom For Crisis Times will give you the answers to the struggle you are facing now, and any struggle you could ever face. Dr. Murdock presents practical steps to help you walk through your "Seasons of Fire."

- ▶ 96 Wisdom Keys from God's Word will direct you into the success that God intended for your life. This teaching will unlock the door to your personal happiness, peace of mind, fulfillment and success.

Wisdom Is The Principal Thing
Book B-40 / $9
Six Audio Tapes TS-69 / $30
The Wisdom Center

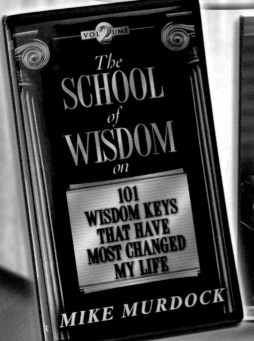
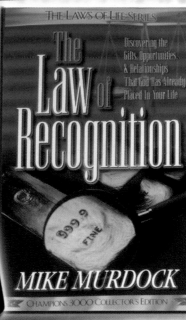

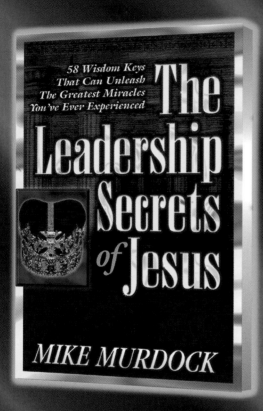

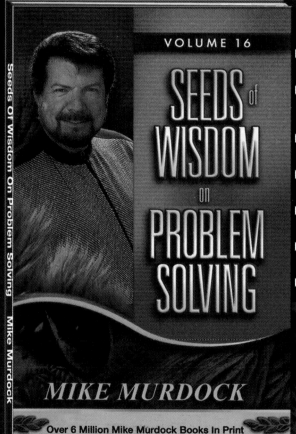

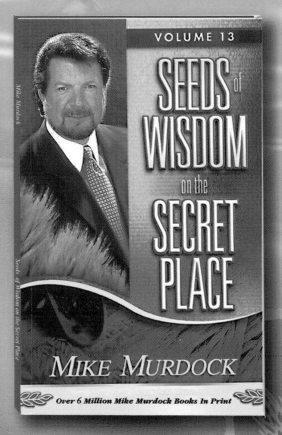

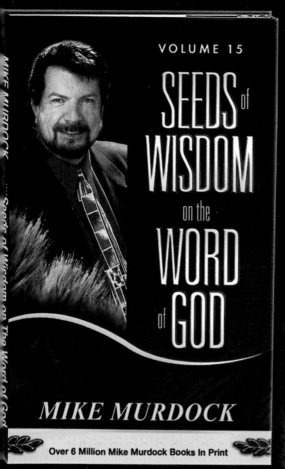

WISDOM COLLECTION

8

SECRETS OF THE UNCOMMON MILLIONAIRE

1. The Uncommon Millionaire Conference Vol. 1 (Six Cassettes)
2. The Uncommon Millionaire Conference Vol. 2 (Six Cassettes)
3. The Uncommon Millionaire Conference Vol. 3 (Six Cassettes)
4. The Uncommon Millionaire Conference Vol. 4 (Six Cassettes)
5. 31 Reasons People Do Not Receive Their
   Financial Harvest (256 Page Book)
6. Secrets of the Richest Man Who Ever Lived
   (178 Page Book)
7. 12 Seeds of Wisdom Books On 12 Topics
8. The Gift of Wisdom for Leaders Desk Calendar
9. Songs From The Secret Place (Music Cassette)
10. In Honor of the Holy Spirit (Music Cassette)
11. 365 Memorization Scriptures On The Word Of God (Audio Cassette)

Wisdom Is The Principal Thing

THE WISDOM COLLECTION 8
SECRETS OF THE UNCOMMON
MILLIONAIRE

WC-08 /$195

The Wisdom Center